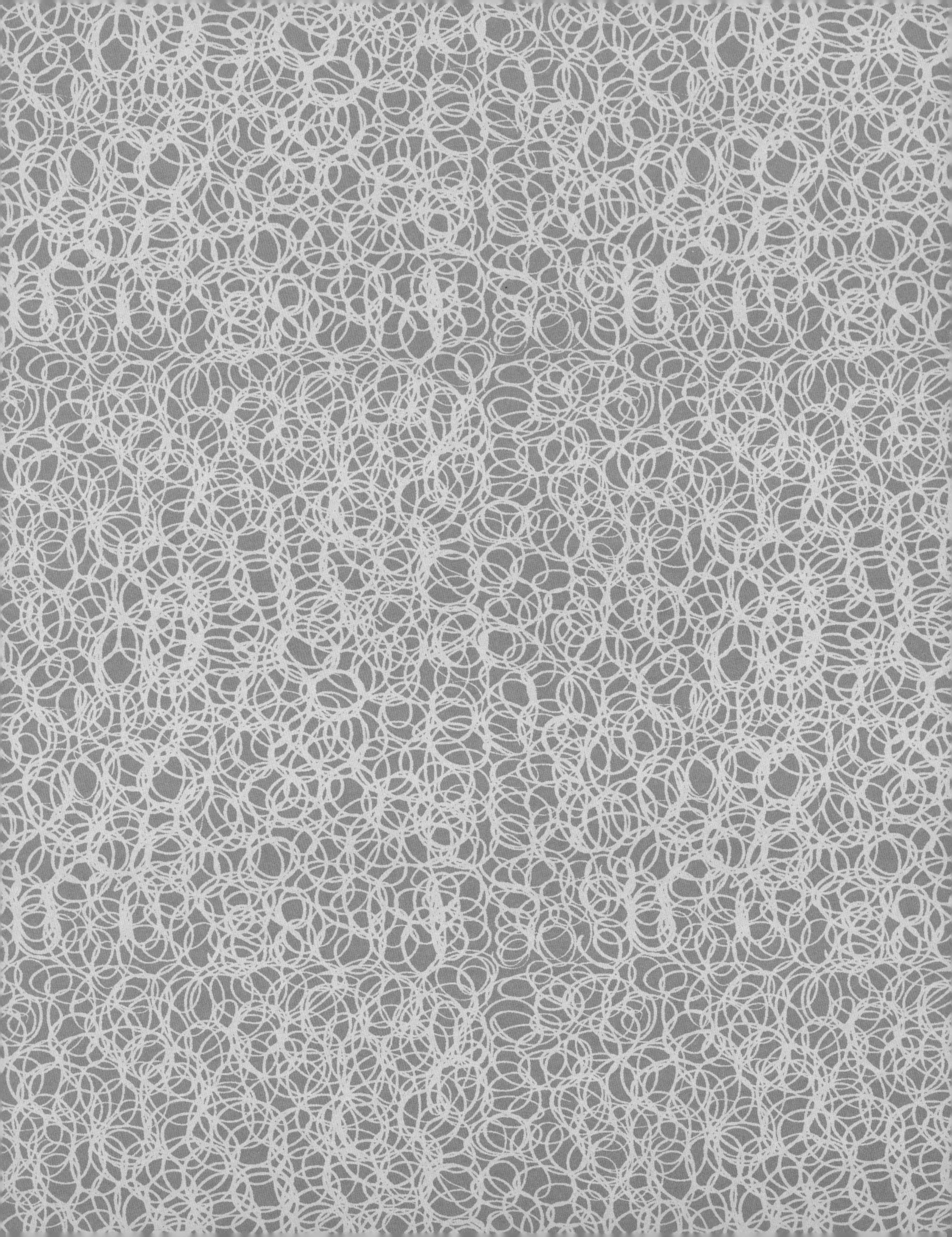

Kindness

written by
Zanni Louise

art by
Missy Turner

FIVE MILE

Hi, I am Jack.
My name
is Lila!
Hola, I am Mina.

I am Li Wei.

I'm Rosie ...

... and this is Freckles!

A big heart helps you care for the world, care for yourself, and care for others.

But how do you grow your heart?

One ingredient you can use to grow your heart is kindness.

What is kindness?

There are many ways to be kind ...

Kindness is being generous.

Lila's dad takes her to the fair. She is especially excited about her balloon.

While Lila's on the ferris wheel her balloon floats away. Lila's happy feeling floats away too.

'You can have my balloon,' says Mina, even though she loves her blue balloon.

Lila hugs her friend.

Kindness is imagining how someone else feels, and reaching out.

Jack reads about older people who are lonely, because their families live far away.

Even though he has never met these people, Jack sends pictures and letters to help them feel less lonely.

Now Jack has six pen pals!

Kindness is taking notice, and taking action.

Rosie is proud.

She has saved so many gold coins! They clink together in her pocket.

But the man on the street looks hungry. She imagines how hard it must be to not have a meal, or a place to live.

Rosie drops her coins into the man's cup.

Later, she sees him warm his hands against a bucket of hot chips.

Sometimes no-one else notices a small act of kindness, but it feels good to be kind.

Li Wei promises to do five kind things each day.

On Tuesday, he collects rubbish in the playground.

He tidies Miss Rachel's desk at lunchtime.

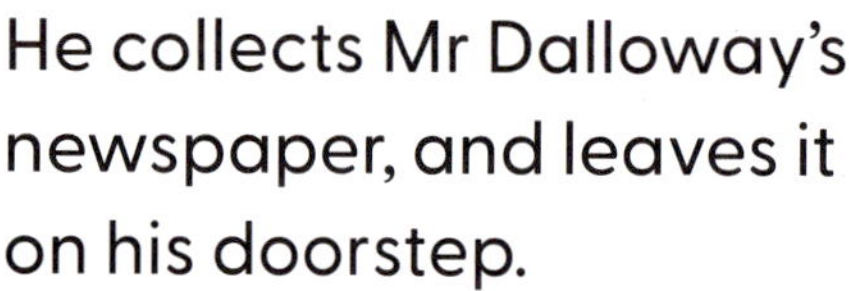

He collects Mr Dalloway's newspaper, and leaves it on his doorstep.

He picks gardenias for Mum because they are her favourite.

And he plants a seed, to grow tomatoes for the birds.

It makes Li Wei feel good to know he was kind.

Kindness is extra special when it makes other people feel good too.

Lila's dad is not well. Lila gives Dad her favourite toy to keep him company.

She writes down all the ways she loves her dad, and leaves the card for him to find.

Lila's dad can't hug her, but he smiles and blows a big kiss from the couch.

Being kind inspires others to be kind.
And that works well for everyone.

Mina has lost the pen she got at the museum. She'll be the only person in class who didn't bring Show and Tell.

'Let me help you,' says Rosie.

They look together.

Soon, the whole class joins in!

They don't find Mina's pen.

But Mina feels much better.

Sometimes you want to be kind. But it takes courage.

Rosie misspells
her name.

Everyone laughs at Rosie.

Only Jack doesn't join in.
He can see Rosie
feels embarrassed.

Jack draws a forest around Rosie's name. Now Rosie has the most interesting name on the board.

Sometimes kindness isn't your first thought. But you can choose kindness.

Mina's sister Juniper has brand new sneakers. Mina is jealous. She wishes she had new sneakers too.

But Mina doesn't like this feeling. So she chooses to do something kind.

'Juni! I drew you a hopscotch. You can test out your new shoes!' says Mina.

It's important to be kind to others. But being kind to yourself is important too.

Lila's new watch is broken. It's full of sand.

She is so cross at herself for being careless.

But she takes a big breath, and takes a new perspective. She would never be cross at her friends for making the same mistake.

Lila decides to treat herself as she would treat her friends. With kindness.

Kindness can mean doing things that make a noticeable difference.

But kindness can also be small and quiet.

Sometimes the only place it's noticed is in our hearts.

Kindness connects us,

and inspires others to do good things too.

Kindness feels right.

And being kind feels good.

Kindness helps your heart grow, so you can look after the world, yourself and each other.

What does kindness
mean to you?

Let's talk about kindness

Can you remember a time when someone was kind?

Lucas performer

'I recently recorded some didgeridoo sounds for a friend's music project. In return, he gifted me with some amazing fresh produce from his garden. Kindness can be shared both ways!'

Zohra writer

'I complimented a lady on her vest at the checkout. She unpacked her trolley, removed her vest, folded it and gave it to me. "I'd like you to have it!" she said. I was amazed at the generosity of a complete stranger!'

Jason carpenter

'When we moved from the US to Australia, our friends gave us a surprise greeting with flowers, coffee, and other treats. One of them even drove 300km to be there! Their kindness helped us know that we were not alone in a new land.'

Carrie managing lawyer

'I had just returned home from hospital after the birth of my first child. We were exhausted and hungry, but there was no food in the house. There was a knock on the door and it was my husband's boss with a hamper of homemade meals that my husband's workmates had cooked for us. I have never felt so grateful!'

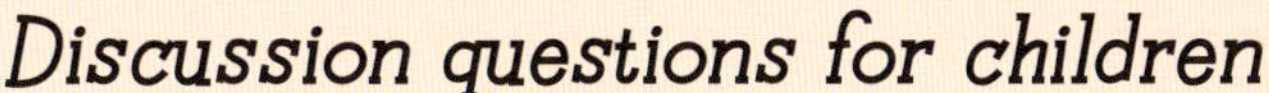

Discussion questions for children

Kindness includes behaviours like giving, helping, sharing, comforting, listening and using kind words.

- What would the world be like if everyone was kind to each other?
- Can you think of a time when you did something kind? How did it feel?
- Who does kind things for you?
- How do you feel when someone is kind to you?
- It's not always easy to be kind, especially when you're feeling grumpy or tired, or things aren't going your way. What can you do to stay calm, so you can be kind?
- Kindness takes practice. What is one kind thing you could do tomorrow?

Notes for parents and carers

Kindness is such an important behaviour for children to learn. Being kind helps children connect with others, regulate their emotions and build healthy relationships. When children treat others with kindness, then people are more likely to be kind to them.

Kindness is what psychologists call a 'prosocial behaviour', a behaviour that benefits others and contributes positively to society.

Kindness and empathy go hand in hand. When children understand how another person feels, they can understand what that person needs. Empathy helps children resolve conflict, consider different perspectives and be kind to people who are different from themselves.

Children may use kindness to relieve the distress of others, to make friends or to gain the approval of caregivers. They may also be kind because it is the 'right' thing to do or simply because it feels good. Whatever the reason, kindness should be encouraged because it helps to build more connected and resilient communities.

Tips for nurturing kindness in children

- Children are more likely to be kind when kindness is valued by their caregivers. When your child has been generous or helpful, describe what you observed and reward the behaviour with lots of positive attention.
- Explain to your child that it is important to be kind to themselves, just as they would be to others. Explore examples of self-compassion and teach them how to assertively express their feelings and needs.
- Model kindness through your own words and actions, by treating yourself and others with kindness and respect.
- Talk about everyday acts of kindness. Point out when others have been kind. Explore kindness through play and storytelling. Show your child that kindness comes in many forms and that even a small act of kindness can make a difference.
- Teach your child empathy skills. Talk about the emotions of others and help them search for emotional clues like facial expressions, body language and tone of voice. Help them identify people who may benefit from some kindness.
- It is hard for children to be kind when they are overwhelmed by emotions. Help your child develop skills to cope with big feelings and stay calm, so they can think clearly and choose kind actions.
- Focus on building a warm, responsive relationship with your child. Children have a greater capacity for empathy and compassion when their own emotional needs are met. They also learn that they are worthy of care and kindness.

Dr Ameika Johnson Child Clinical Psychologist

Also available in this book series

Honesty

Honesty is talking to yourself and others truthfully. Honesty brings us closer, keeps us safer and helps people trust us. Honesty is not always easy. Sometimes it's the hardest choice.

There are many ways to be honest ...

Persistence

Persistence is never giving up, even when things get tough. Persistence helps us try new things, get better at hard things, and cope when things get difficult. Persistence helps us see things through to the end.

There are many ways to be persistent ...

Courage

Courage is stepping towards things we think are scary or difficult. Courage helps us find out what we like, what we're good at and shows us that mistakes are okay. Being courageous is not always easy, it can sometimes feel risky.

There are many ways to be courageous...

Made with love by the team at

FIVE MILE

Alex, Niki, Rocco, Graham, Jacqui, Andy, Amy, Lyndal & Emily

Five Mile,
the publishing division
of Regency Media
www.fivemile.com.au

First published 2021

A catalogue record for this book is available from the National Library of Australia

Printed in China 5 4